CANDLE MAGIC

AN ENCHANTING SPELL BOOK OF CANDLES AND RITUALS

Minerva Radcliffe

wellfleet
press

Introduction

Wax, wick, and flame: Three simple ingredients, yet they combine to make the ever-ubiquitous candle. Candles have been in use since 200 BCE, and their candor and practicality are why we use them today. They light our homes, guide us through the darkness, and in witchcraft, allow us to be closer to the Divine; they act as a beacon for the Universe to come our way, to aid us, and to teach us.

Fire, the candle's companion, is the element of passion, purpose, energy, and motivation. It is similar to water as they both have emotional characteristics rather than the logic and practicality of earth and air. Fire is used for warmth, creation, and destruction. It even has its own holiday—the Summer Solstice, also known as the Fire Festival.

Fire is like a free spirit. It can go from struggling tinder to a monstrous wildfire in seconds. Candles are the balance between fire and the Divine. Some witches say scrying the

flames will reveal a message from the Universe. The candle and the flame work hand in hand, as we do with Spirit. It is an anchor for the flame to center and focus, to be still and give light. Candles have much to offer any witch of all skill levels.

Within these pages, you will find new ways to utilize candles in your own practice, and perhaps you'll combine these spells with your own. As with all witchcraft, these spells are meant to be adjusted to your personal purposes or supplies you have on hand. When reading, take what you need and add what you must. Most importantly, continue to learn and grow, and see what Spirit has in store for you. Be open, be safe, be magical, be powerful. You are made of magic, and that means this book is for *you*.

In order to properly utilize this spell book, there are a few steps you must always perform *before* proceeding with a spell. The first is to create a magic circle. A magic circle is similar

to closing the door of a room. It prevents anything from entering your space so that you may work in peace. It helps to focus your attention on the present moment and not on what may or may not come through the "door" so to speak. Create your circle by using your wand or your finger to draw a circle around your space, like an energy shield.

The second is to cleanse your space. Many witches use incense, burn sage or palo santo, or use a concocted herbal spray. This ensures no unwanted influences interfere with your practice. At times, we may not realize we are carrying others' baggage, or we might have some lingering magic on us we must be rid of. It is imperative to be clean and clear when practicing our craft. Cover the entire space with either the smoke or spray, using the cleansing tool of your choice. Do not skip any corner or entryway.

The third is to settle in. To rid yourself of excessive energy, some witches dance or sing to get it all out before working on a spell. For other witches, this means sitting in stillness and waiting for the mind to calm down. Others use deep breathing exercises to force the mind into an alpha wave state, the perfect state for meditative practice or to receive messages from the Universe. Use your intuition and do what is right for you. The time to thrive is now.

So mote it be.*

*The term "So mote it be" used within is a ritual phrase historically used by Freemasons, and currently used by Neopagan practitioners translated to mean "So it must be."

Color
Magic

THE WORLD AROUND US IS painted in color. Colors can create a sense of comfort, bring joy, stimulate the senses, and soothe anxiety. Colored candles carry significant meanings, strengthening spell work.

Red is the color of passion and survival. Pink is for friendship and love. Orange is for positivity. Yellow is for joy and happiness. Green is for luck. Blue promotes calm and intuition. Purple represents psychic abilities. Brown is for grounding yourself in the present moment. Black is for protection, and white is the catch-all color but also symbolizes purity.

In this chapter, you will utilize each color to harvest its magical properties. Colors act as unspoken words during the spell. They tell the Universe your intention as they give off their own magical energy. Think of the colors of your candles as another layer of meanings in your spells. They have much to give, and you have much to gain from their presence. As you go through this chapter, you will learn their deeper meanings. Colored candles are a perfect addition to strengthen any spell you intend to perform. Use them wisely and let them guide you.

White Candle Meditation

In magic, white is the universal color. It can represent any color you wish but it also stands for purity and unity. If you're new to candle magic, white candles are the best place to begin. This meditation will help you familiarize yourself with candle magic as a whole.

Necessary components: ♦ At least 1 white candle

♦ A comfortable place to sit

♦ Music (optional)

Set your intention for what you want out of this candle. Turn on some music that will help you concentrate if you wish. Light your candle and sit while focusing on the flame and how it sways or sparks. Close your eyes and think about what you want to glean from this experience. As you meditate, silently chant these words:

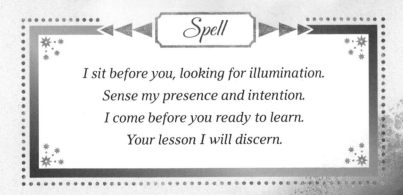

Spell

I sit before you, looking for illumination.
Sense my presence and intention.
I come before you ready to learn.
Your lesson I will discern.

Honor the Dark Moon

There are approximately nine phases of the Moon: New Moon, Waxing Crescent, First Quarter, Waxing Gibbous, Full Moon, Waning Gibbous, Last Quarter, Waning Crescent, and finally, the Dark Moon. The Dark Moon is the gestation period between death and birth. The Dark Moon represents the darkness in all of us. Instead of fearing it, it is important to embrace and honor the darkness within. After all, without the dark, how can we see the light?

Necessary components:

- ♦ 1 large black candle to represent the Dark Moon
- ♦ Your book of shadows and a pen
- ♦ A clear view of the night sky

Light your candle where you can see it and the sky simultaneously. In your book of shadows, reflect on the necessity of darkness in both the Moon and you. Once you are done, look up at the sky and say:

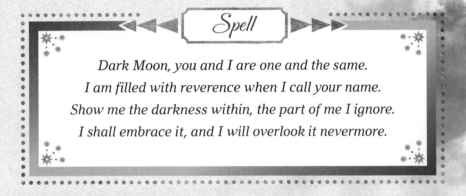

Spell

Dark Moon, you and I are one and the same.
I am filled with reverence when I call your name.
Show me the darkness within, the part of me I ignore.
I shall embrace it, and I will overlook it nevermore.

Perform this spell during each Dark Moon phase of the month.

Indecision Begone!

There are moments in this life when we are faced with two options but only one choice. Sitting with indecision does nothing but halt our lives and prevent us from attaining what we deserve or need. Use this spell before making a final decision.

Gather:

♦ 1 black candle to represent the primary choice

♦ 1 white candle to represent the secondary choice

♦ 1 gray candle to represent your indecision

♦ 3 small pieces of tissue paper

♦ Tongs and a pen

♦ A fireproof dish

1. Set up your altar and arrange the candles from left to right: black, gray, and white.

2. On two of the pieces of tissue paper, inscribe your two main choices. Place each decision in front of the corresponding candle.

3. On the third piece, write down why you are hesitating with this choice, then place that piece in front of the gray candle.

4. Close your eyes and imagine the outcome of both choices. Do not judge what you think; simply let your mind pour over the choices. Consult with your patron deity.

5. Once you have made your choice, use the tongs to burn all three papers with their corresponding candles *except* your final decision.

6. Burn the final paper with the gray candle. Let the paper burn out in the fireproof dish and let the gray candle burn out.

You are indecisive no more. So mote it be.

Home Blessing Candle Spell

Home is our safe place, where we practice our craft. There are many things we cannot control, but we *can* control how we move about in our space. Without a dwelling, life would be much harder, so use this spell as a blessing to your faithful home.

Gather:

♦ 6 brown candles for blessing the home (or you can use 1 brown candle with a number 6 carved on it)

♦ Selenite (preferably a wand) for cleansing

Wave your selenite throughout your home, paying special attention to corners. When you are done, place the brown candles in the major areas of your home, like your bedroom or the living room, and light them. Once all candles have been lit, recite this spell:

Spell

I cleanse you, house, and make you anew.
May this wand and spell be true.
May this blessing be full and may it last
Long after this spell was cast.

Meet Your Animal Totem

The word "totem" comes from the Ojibwe culture and refers to an animal that is a spirit guide in the form of a living creature, also known as your familiar. In this spell, you will discover how to discover, and form a bond with your totem.

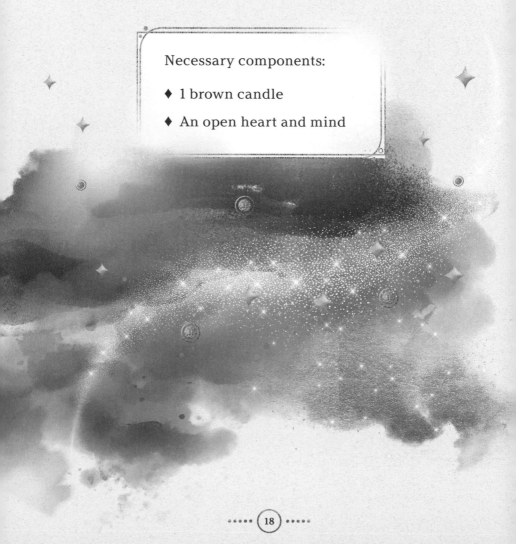

Necessary components:

♦ 1 brown candle

♦ An open heart and mind

1. Place the brown candle on your altar. Your intention is to have the spirit come to you without preconceived notions.

2. Close your eyes and imagine yourself in a field alone.

3. Wait for a sign. It might be a whoosh of wind, you may feel movement around you, or maybe your intuition stirs. When this happens, ask the spirit who they are, and let them reveal themselves to you.

How you proceed beyond this point is up to you but remember to keep an open mind. Be present and respectful. When you are done, thank them for their presence, and their protection.

Invigorate the Soul

In the society we live in, we must work, work, work, making it easy to fall into a rut. It's tempting to cope by living life on autopilot so that we don't have to do anything we don't want to. With this spell, you will invigorate your body and soul so that you can move forward, feeling fortified instead of numb.

Necessary components:

♦ 2 red candles, one for the body and one for the soul

♦ Moisture-wicking clothes

♦ A towel to wipe your face

♦ Uplifting music (optional)

1. Light the red candles and move to the center of your space.

2. Take a deep breath in, then exhale. Stretch your body and feel your blood flow.

3. Now start moving. You are here in the material world, not a slave to your duties. Allow the red to inspire a passion for life. Say aloud:

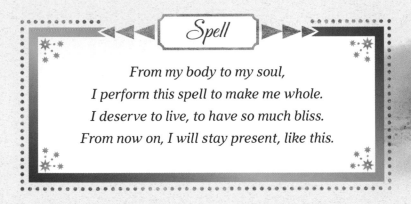

Spell

From my body to my soul,
I perform this spell to make me whole.
I deserve to live, to have so much bliss.
From now on, I will stay present, like this.

Once you have calmed, open your arms to the Universe, breathe in life, and breathe out the monotony.

Broken Heart No More

Some of us know the pain of a broken heart all too well. Pain does not last forever. This spell will aid you in your healing journey and guide you out of the darkness and into the light once more.

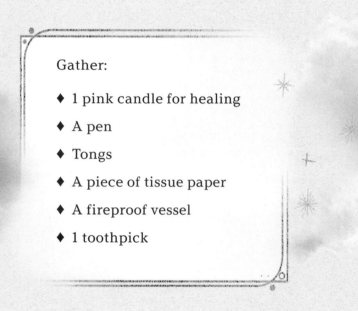

Gather:

♦ 1 pink candle for healing

♦ A pen

♦ Tongs

♦ A piece of tissue paper

♦ A fireproof vessel

♦ 1 toothpick

1. Use the toothpick and carve either your name or initials on the candle.

2. Light the candle and set it on your altar.

3. Sit with your eyes closed and think about the source of your pain. Focus long enough to boil down your heartbreak to one word.

4. On the tissue paper, write down your word.

5. Hold the paper in your hands for a moment and imagine that all your hurt is being transferred onto it. Hold the paper with the tongs and say quietly or aloud:

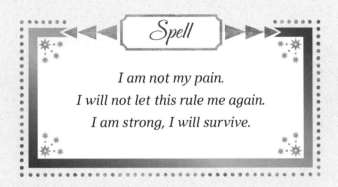

Spell

I am not my pain.
I will not let this rule me again.
I am strong, I will survive.

6. Light the paper on the flame and allow it to burn out in the fireproof dish, then let your candle burn out.

A Burst of Positivity

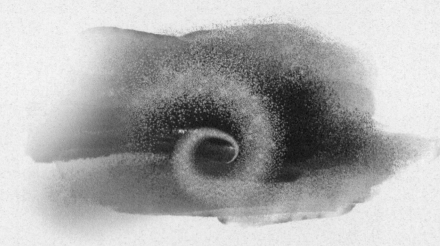

It can be hard to maintain positivity all the time. This spell is meant to remind you of the positives in your life and the good that may come.

Necessary components:

♦ At least 1 orange candle to represent positivity

♦ A comfortable place to sit

♦ Uplifting or calming music

1. Arrange your altar with the orange candle and light it. Play the music and allow yourself to be washed in it.

2. Look at the flame and let your mind slowly drift.

3. Focus your mind and think of three things you are grateful for.

4. Next, name three compliments you have been given and believe them.

5. Close your eyes, smile, and picture a light shining down on you, filling you with the burst of positivity you need.

Open your eyes. You have now completed the spell.

Royal Confidence

Confidence can be difficult to master. Self-assurance is not easy to achieve but it can be done with the right tactics. In this spell, you will conjure up the self-esteem you need to move through your day with the poise and grace of a royal.

Gather:

♦ 1 yellow candle to represent confidence

♦ A wand (you may also use your finger)

1. Arrange your altar with the candle and light it.

2. Stand where you can move in big motions without knocking anything over.

3. Take three deep breaths and let each inhale light your ego, and each exhale expel insecurities.

4. Lift your wand toward the sky. Imagine Spirit sending light to you and through your wand, like an antenna. Coat yourself in it.

5. Use your wand to draw a crown around your head.

6. Feel your new crown of light and say aloud:

◄◄◄ *Spell* ►►►

I am royalty.
Nothing can bring me down.

Grow, Grow, Grow

With growth comes change. Looking at our areas of improvement can be unpleasant and intimidating. Regardless, we must all embrace changes in ourselves in order to thrive. Without change, everything would become stale. We must continue developing to become the best versions of ourselves, and this spell will facilitate that.

Gather:

♦ 1 green candle to represent your evolution

♦ A pen

♦ Your book of light (or a diary)

1. Arrange your altar and light the candle.

2. In your book of light, write down areas in which you'd like to grow.

3. Take a moment to gaze at the flame. Watch it flicker, spark, thin, and expand. The flame is representative of the journey we must all go through.

4. Picture yourself growing taller with change.

5. Breathe in knowing your journey has just begun.

Banish Envy

Envy is an ugly, yet normal emotion. There may be others who give in to envy and then make it your problem. In those times, it is important to know it has nothing to do with you and everything to do with them. With this spell, you will banish envy and keep your peace of mind.

Gather:

♦ 1 green candle to represent envy

♦ A picture or representation of yourself

♦ A picture or representation of the envious person

1. Arrange your altar in order from left to right: picture of yourself, the green candle, and the picture of the other person.

2. Place a hand over the envious person and imagine their energy pooling in your palm.

3. Place your hand over your picture and imagine putting a shield of light over yourself.

4. Take the envy energy and shoot it toward the flame of the candle. Picture it sparking, then dissipating. With that, you have banished the evil energy.

What Is the Truth?

Some believe there is such a thing as universal truth. Others believe truth is subjective and therefore, not something one can easily grasp. Regardless of the stance, some of the clearest truths we have are those we keep within ourselves. However, there are moments when we don't want to acknowledge those facts. We may be too afraid or may not want to face something we know is real. Using this spell, you will find the truth you've been hiding from.

Necessary components:

♦ 1 blue candle to represent the truth within

♦ Calming music

Arrange your altar with the candle and sit so you will be in its light. Light the candle, turn on the calming music, and settle into the moment. Slow your thoughts and focus within. Say quietly or aloud:

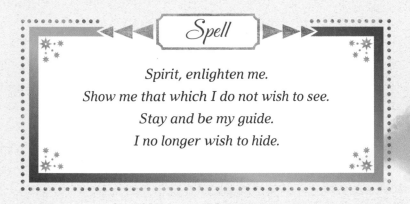

Spell

Spirit, enlighten me.
Show me that which I do not wish to see.
Stay and be my guide.
I no longer wish to hide.

Close your eyes and wait. Your truth will make itself known to you. Once it does, face it with courage. You will be all right. After the moment has passed, thank Spirit for their wisdom and thank yourself for wanting to learn more, no matter the difficulty.

Restore Faith

There are moments in your witchy life where you might question yourself or abilities. Perhaps you have gone through a dry period where your petitions to the Universe have been met with denials. Maybe you have been unable to practice due to mental blocks. Whatever the source, know it is possible to regain faith in yourself and your abilities.

Gather:

♦ 1 purple candle for faithfulness

♦ A pen and your book of light

♦ A standalone mirror

1. Arrange your altar and place the candle in front of the mirror.

2. In your book of light, inscribe your thoughts.

3. Gaze at yourself in the mirror and look yourself in the eye. As you do this, ask yourself why you feel doubtful and how to overcome it. Say quietly or aloud:

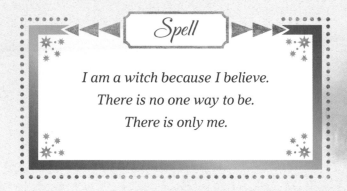

Spell

I am a witch because I believe.
There is no one way to be.
There is only me.

Smile at yourself and rest in the knowledge that you are enough.

Attract Success

Success can be achieved, especially if you have the sun working in your favor. In this spell, you will call upon the powers of the sun to aid you in your quest for success. Remember that success is not instantaneous; it's something that comes over time and with discipline.

Gather:

- ◆ 1 gold candle to represent the Sun
- ◆ A physical representation of your goal
- ◆ Red, orange, yellow, or gold clothing

1. Don yourself with the color-themed clothing. The colors are symbolic of the Sun and will help add extra intention to the spell.

2. Arrange your altar with the gold candle and light it.

3. Hold the representation of your goal in your hand. Imagine your energy pouring into it and picture what it would be like to achieve it. Look up toward the sky and say this quietly or aloud:

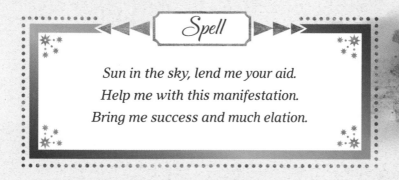

Spell

Sun in the sky, lend me your aid.
Help me with this manifestation.
Bring me success and much elation.

4. Place your representation in front of the candle so that it can be bathed in its light.

Lunar Empowerment Spell

The Moon is a wise and powerful entity. In moments when you feel powerless or under attack, it's time to call upon Mother Moon for guidance and empowerment.

Necessary components:

♦ 1 silver candle to represent the Moon

♦ A full view of the Moon (a picture will suffice)

♦ Empowering music

♦ Gray or silver clothing

1. Do a brief meditation, don themed clothes or you may even add accessories; anything to get you in the proper headspace.

2. Next, arrange your altar and light the candle. Turn on your music. With a clear view of the Moon, recite these words quietly or aloud:

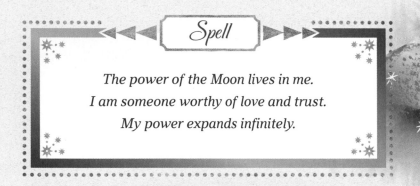

Spell

The power of the Moon lives in me.
I am someone worthy of love and trust.
My power expands infinitely.

Now, move about your space in time with the music. Soak in the words of the spell and let it propel you forward. Any positive thought that comes to mind, let it come and accept it as fact. You have gone through so much in life and you are still standing. You are strong. Remember that.

Melted Wax Seal

One of the most effective forms of witchcraft is the spell jar. Spell jars can be used for virtually anything from curses, enchantments, or blessings. The way to ensure the jar stays powerful is to properly seal it. It sounds simple, but unlike the spells readily available online, this spell takes more than just letting a candle melt over a cork.

Necessary components:

♦ 1 candle with a color that reflects your intention

♦ 1 or more spell jars

♦ A steady hand and a watchful eye

1. Take a spell jar and wrap your hands around it. Imagine it glowing as you hold it.

2. Light your candle of choice and then tilt it so it's horizontal. Let the wax drip onto the bottle. Turn the candle around little by little so there's an even melt all around. Keep going until the whole cork is covered and there are streaks down the side for that classic look.

Honoring Both Sides
of the Divine

The interesting thing about Spirit and the Universe is that they have many sides to them. There is no gender exactly, but there are masculine and feminine aspects to their power. We all have aspects of each binary within us. With this spell, you will honor both sides of the Divine and honor them in yourself.

Gather:

♦ 1 gold (or yellow) candle to represent the masculine side

♦ 1 silver (or gray) candle to represent the feminine side

♦ A pen

♦ Your book of light (or a diary)

1. Arrange both candles on your altar and light them.

2. In your book of light, inscribe in two columns, the masculine and feminine aspects of the Divine, and then add your own qualities to them.

3. Take a moment to reflect on how similar you are to Spirit with all of your many qualities. Close your eyes and then say quietly or aloud:

Spell

Today I honor the energy in you
and the energy in me.

Welcome Home, Nature

Part of being a witch is bringing pieces of nature home with you. Even though the natural world is at our disposal, it does not mean it is ours to take. Instead, we must acknowledge where each item came from and welcome it into our homes.

Gather:

♦ 1 brown candle to represent the earth

♦ 1 green candle to represent the flora

♦ 1 gold candle to represent the Sun

♦ The retrieved object

1. Arrange your altar with the candles from left to right in this order: brown, gold, and green.

2. Light all three candles and then place the object in front of the gold candle. Take a moment to examine this item. Why did you choose it? Did it choose you?

3. Hold the object in your hand and ask it if it would like to live with you.

4. If you receive a no, put it back where you found it. If yes, hold it near the flame and say:

Spell

As you have received me, so have I received you.
Welcome to my home.

Time to Heal

Long gone are the days of practicing witchcraft in caves or cottages. Instead, we are a part of the modern world which comes with modern stress. Sometimes we need to slow down and focus on repairing ourselves so that we may conquer any situation we face.

Necessary components:

♦ 5 white candles for healing and regeneration

♦ Soothing music

♦ A familiar (optional)

♦ Your favorite drink

1. Place the candles all about your space so that the room is lit up with a warm glow.

2. Turn on your music and cuddle up with your familiar if you choose to have one.

3. Sit in the middle of the space and stir your drink in a deosil (clockwise) motion.

4. Now, perform a mental scan of your body to see where you need the most healing. Say quietly or aloud:

Spell

Flames, bathe me in your glow.
Ground me in my feeling.
Touch the parts I know need the most healing.

Communicate with Your Higher Self

No one knows you better than yourself. In times when you feel like you've lost yourself, you must consult with your Higher Self. It's crucial that we communicate with our Higher Selves as often as we can. This is the most evolved part of yourself and can always be trusted to enlighten you.

Necessary components:

♦ 1 blue candle to represent your intuition

♦ 1 gray candle to represent your higher self

♦ A comfortable place to sit

♦ Calming music (optional)

1. Arrange your altar and light the candles. If using music, turn it on.

2. Begin your meditative state, starting from the root chakra and moving up to the sacral chakra, solar plexus, heart, throat, third eye, and then crown chakra.

3. Ask your Higher Self what messages you need to receive.

It may take some time before you hear something but have patience. It'll come.

2

Number Magic

THERE IS POWER IN NUMBERS. They are the building blocks to understanding the physical world, and are a part of our everyday lives without us even thinking about them too much.

What many do not know is that numbers hold an ancient power, have their own specific qualities, they use feminine, masculine, and nonbinary energy, and they can tell us much about ourselves. Acknowledging the power of numbers is called numerology. As you look through the pages of this chapter, you will see how numbers affect your material world *and* your spiritual world. This chapter uses the fire and colors of candles paired with the power of individual root numbers, triad number combinations, and angel numbers— messages from divine beings.

At the end of the chapter, you will use sacred geometry, which is defined as the geometry that exists in Nature. The golden ratio is a perfect example of this concept. Because it is a naturally occurring phenomenon, we could say numbers are a part of the physical world and, therefore, a part of us. Use these pages to gain a deeper understanding of the potency of pairing numbers with your candles to add firepower to your spells.

Amass Zero's Unique Power

When written properly, zero is a complete and perfect circle, representing eternity. In this spell, you will open the portal within zero and harness its unique power.

Gather:

♦ 5 white candles for the light aspect of 0

♦ 5 black candles for the infinite possibilities of 0

♦ A wand

1. Arrange the candles around you in a perfect circle in the order of white then black.

2. Point your wand at the lit candles, then move in a circle starting from east to north, then west then south, so that you cover all the directions. As you move, say:

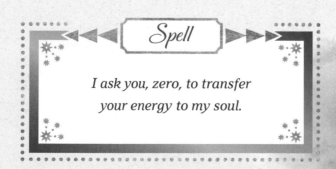

Spell

*I ask you, zero, to transfer
your energy to my soul.*

1: Spring into Action

The energy of one is constantly moving, making whoever summons it become energetic too. It activates the mind to come up with ideas that are ready to be acted upon. One's focus is on getting work done and achieving goals. If you have been waiting for inspiration, the number one will bring it.

Gather:

♦ 1 red candle for passion and willpower

♦ A small piece of tissue paper and a pen

1. Arrange your altar with the red candle and light it.

2. Take your pen and draw a long, straight line.

3. Next, take your paper and place it in front of the candle but do not stop touching it. This will allow the energy to flow from the paper to you.

Close your eyes and then think of what you need to accomplish. Feel one's energy move from your fingertips, up your arms, and throughout your body. Use this to grasp the power and see in your mind's eye that you have already achieved your goals.

2: Imagination

Having a colorful imagination has been proven to preserve memory, help with problem solving, foster empathy, and inspire us to think outside the box. The number two understands this well, and those whose root number is two tend to be more internally focused and, therefore, more imaginative. In this spell, you will employ the attributes of two to your advantage.

Gather:

♦ 2 gray candles for balance

♦ Your book of light (or a diary) and a pen

1. Arrange your altar with the candles and light them.

2. Draw a 2, then let your imagination run wild. Write as much as you can; don't hold anything back. The entire point is to simply think. If you get stuck or blocked, put two fingers on the 2 and absorb power from that.

When you are done, take a look at what you have come up with and what it says about you. Do this in times of low inspiration.

3: Have Some Fun

There are moments in our craft and our lives when everything just feels too serious. It is important to have fun every now and again to get some relief from the grind. Three consists of two semicircles joined together at one point in the middle. The two halves are open to receive and release. This spell will allow you to bask in the lightness of the moment.

Necessary components:

♦ 3 yellow candles for joy

♦ A silly accessory, like a pinwheel or a slinky

♦ Upbeat music

1. Arrange your altar with the candles and light them.

2. Turn on the music and dance. Be wild and unrestricted!

3. Once you tire from dancing, grab your silly accessory and play with it. Become a child with no worries or cares. Lose yourself in the moment!

4. When you feel yourself begin to slow down, blow out the candles and rest.

4: Plan Your Self-Care

The number four is about mindfulness. Its energies, and those whose root number is four, are skewed toward preparation. Because we are constantly busy doing what needs to be done, we may not always make time or plan for self-care. It is all too easy to put self-care to the side and ignore our needs. But it is a necessity. Use four to achieve this.

Gather:

♦ 4 blue candles

♦ A pen

♦ Your book of light (or a diary)

♦ A planner

1. Arrange your altar with the four candles and light them. Write down the ways you enjoy self-care.

2. Next, write what the necessary components are for your self-care and where you can get them. This helps to see where your limitations are and where you might need to get creative.

3. Last, use your enchanted planner to set a date, preferably a day with a four in it. For better results, try to do a multi-day process so you can get all the rest you need.

4. When you are finished, draw fours in your planner to get aid from the number itself.

Now, go enjoy yourself.

5: Using Your Inherent Charm

Although five is an odd number, it is the building block to many even numbers. In this way, five has a unique position within numerology: It is both feminine and masculine in nature, reflecting its flexibility. Just like five, we are walking contradictions and that is what makes us charming. For this spell, let five highlight the charm in you. In numerology, five is written out with two straight lines and a semicircle. The energy exerts itself up and down, left to right, and the semicircle catches everything the Universe offers.

Gather:

♦ 5 orange candles for attraction from others

♦ A pen

♦ A piece of parchment paper

Arrange your altar with the candles and light them. Draw a 5 as described on the previous page, with two straight lines and a semicircle, on the parchment paper. As you draw, recite these words five times quietly or aloud:

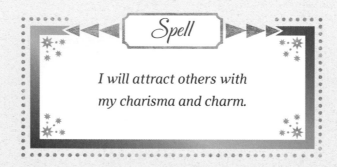

Spell

I will attract others with my charisma and charm.

Carry the parchment paper on your person and go about your day. Notice how much more people will open up to you.

555: Life Changes Spell

Angel numbers are a subsect of numerology, the relationship between numbers and the Divine. If you've seen the numbers 555 lately, it could be an omen that life changes are coming. With this spell, you will honor the angel who sent you the numbers and prepare for the change on the horizon.

Gather:

♦ 5 candles (or you can use 3 candles with a 5 carved on each one)

♦ 1 toothpick

Set up your altar however you wish. After doing so, light all the candles, sit comfortably, and recite this incantation:

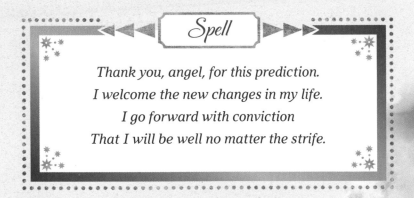

Spell

Thank you, angel, for this prediction.
I welcome the new changes in my life.
I go forward with conviction
That I will be well no matter the strife.

666: Rid Your Mind of Negative Thinking

Instead of letting negative thoughts linger, be rid of them. If you have been seeing 666 lately, it is a sign that you *must* change your thinking to restore balance. In numerology, sixes are written as a complete circle with curved line from the circle, meaning the infinite possibilities of the circle are grounded by the line. With this spell, you'll unravel the harmful thought patterns you may find yourself stuck in.

Gather:

♦ 6 black candles to absorb negative energy

1. Arrange your altar with the black candles. Light them and sit in a comfortable position.

2. Close your eyes and take a few deep breaths.

3. Gently examine your negative thoughts. Did someone give them to you, or did you give them to yourself?

4. While saying this spell, envision the number 666 and call upon your angels, your patron deity, or Spirit. Recite these words six times quietly or aloud:

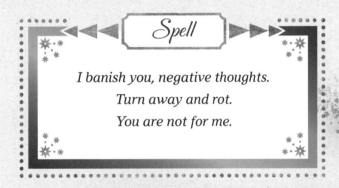

Spell

I banish you, negative thoughts.
Turn away and rot.
You are not for me.

When completed, open your eyes and thank your guardians for their help.

777: Celebrate!

When you see 777 in your life, it means you are doing an excellent job! This is a sign that good things are coming your way. So, take a moment to rejoice! To properly draw a seven, draw one line diagonally, then add a second line at the top. With this spell, you will celebrate with your guardian and acknowledge your own hard work.

Necessary components:

♦ 3 orange candles for celebration

♦ 1 toothpick

♦ Happy music

♦ Iconography of your guardian/deity

♦ Any potions or morsels you desire

1. Turn on the happy music and then arrange your altar with the three candles.

2. With the toothpick, inscribe the number 7 on each candle. Then light them.

3. Take the iconography and place it wherever you wish, as long as it is easily seen. You may even invite them to celebrate with you.

Now, eat, drink, and be merry! Dance as much as you wish, drink until your heart's content, and enjoy the moment. You earned it.

888: Prosperity Is Coming

If you have been seeing 888 lately, it means financial gains are coming into your life soon. The number eight on its own consists of two perfect circles, one on top of the other. This means energy is constantly flowing from one circle to the next in a wondrous loop.

With this spell, you will manifest your financial goals.

Gather:

♦ 3 green candles for money

♦ 1 toothpick

♦ The Eight of Pentacles tarot card

♦ Physical money, like bills or coins

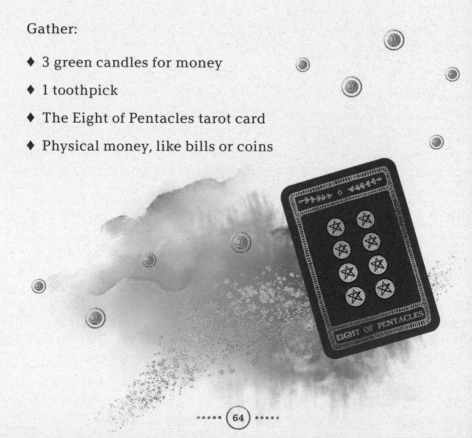

1. Use the toothpick to carve an 8 on each candle. Arrange them on your altar and then light them.

2. Scatter the money along the altar and hold the tarot card in your hand.

3. Close your eyes and imagine the light from the candles illuminating the 8s carved into them. Picture that light shining on the cash dispersed about your altar.

4. Next, take the Eight of Pentacles card and gaze into it. Say this incantation eight times:

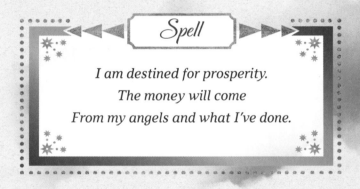

Spell

I am destined for prosperity.
The money will come
From my angels and what I've done.

5. If you wish, carry the tarot card and some of the bills on your person as an extra boost.

999: Time for a Change

The number nine is the final and highest root number in numerology. It signifies the end. This could be the end of a relationship, career, or chapter in your life. If you see 999, it means you are being called to change direction. Nine comprises two shapes: a perfect circle and a single downward line. The circle represents the endless possibilities your new path contains. The line represents your place in all this—a person grounded in reality. Combined, they form a vision for the future.

Gather:

♦ 3 black candles for positive changes through difficult times

♦ 1 toothpick

1. Use the toothpick to carve a 9 on each candle.

2. Arrange your altar with the candles, then light them. Find a comfortable place to sit and play music if you wish.

3. Take three deep breaths and let your mind become clear.

4. Ask yourself what in your life no longer serves you.

5. Open your third eye and recite this incantation quietly or aloud:

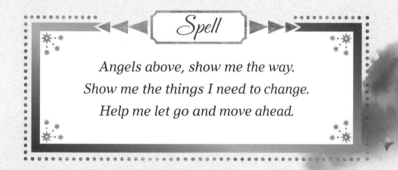

Spell

Angels above, show me the way.
Show me the things I need to change.
Help me let go and move ahead.

When you have your answer, open your eyes and thank your angel.

1010: A Spiritual Awakening Is Coming

Our bodies do not make us who we are, our souls do, and they need to be tended to. If you are seeing 1010 often, this is a sign from your angels that you need to pay more attention to your spiritual self. Once you do, you will experience a spiritual awakening.

Gather:

♦ 4 white candles

♦ 1 toothpick

1. Use the toothpick to inscribe the number 1 on two candles and 0 on the other two. Arrange them on your altar and light them.

2. Sit and close your eyes. Look within and gaze upon your soul. Scan it to find out where it needs attention. Once you have identified the correct points, your angel will tell you what you need and guide you to your awakening.

Mind, Body, and Soul Candle Formation

A trinity taps into your mind, body, and soul. If you've ever felt out of sync but couldn't quite place it, this spell will help you align and unify all parts of yourself.

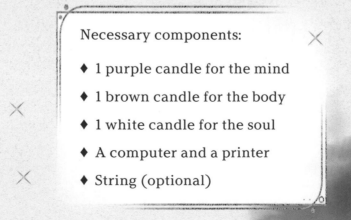

Necessary components:

♦ 1 purple candle for the mind

♦ 1 brown candle for the body

♦ 1 white candle for the soul

♦ A computer and a printer

♦ String (optional)

1. Begin by identifying which aspects of you are out of sync. When you have done so, take the candles of your choice and touch each one to the corresponding points on your body: your forehead for your mind, your stomach for your body, and your heart for your soul.

2. Now, place the candles on your altar in a triangle. If you do not have a printer, use string to connect the candles. Say this incantation quietly or aloud:

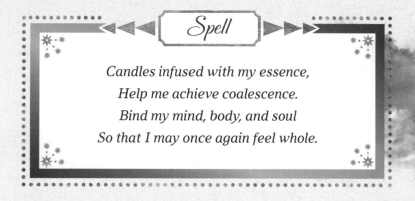

Spell

Candles infused with my essence,
Help me achieve coalescence.
Bind my mind, body, and soul
So that I may once again feel whole.

Imagine all the parts of you coming together as it did with the string and feel complete once again.

Energy-Organized Square

The square is the foundation of so many structures; they gather the energy of the cosmos, hold it, and then organize it down here on earth. If you feel as though you have built-up energy, this spell will help you sort it and send energy to where it is needed.

Necessary components:

♦ 4 brown candles for grounding

♦ A computer with a printer

♦ Straight objects, like sticks or pens (optional)

1. On your computer, find a basic square shape. If you don't have a printer, use sticks or other similar objects to connect the candles.

2. Arrange the candles on the square so that they are sitting on each corner and light them.

3. Close your eyes and do a scan of your body. Where is the energy built up in you? Once you have identified the origin, hover your hands on that point.

4. Direct this energy to the candles and watch the flame dance. Picture the energy going from you into the flame, down the candle, and onto the paper. Imagine the square glowing, taking in your movements. With hands extended, say quietly:

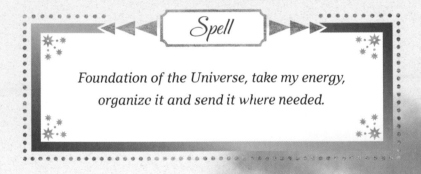

Spell

Foundation of the Universe, take my energy,
organize it and send it where needed.

It is in Spirit's hands now.

Searching for Freedom

There are moments in every witch's life where they feel trapped or stuck. In this spell, we will look at the hexagon, the six-sided shape. In sacred geometry, the hexagon symbolizes abundance and freedom. If you are feeling trapped in your situation, this is one way to take control.

Necessary components:

♦ 6 black candles for escaping unwanted situations

♦ A computer with a printer

♦ Straight objects, like sticks or pens (optional)

♦ An athame

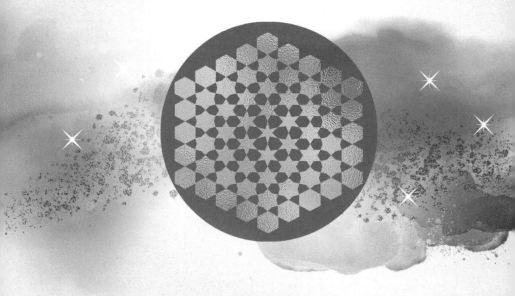

1. On your computer, find a picture of a hexagon. Arrange your altar and place each candle on the corners of the hexagon. If you do not have a printer, you may use sticks or other straight objects to create the shape. Light the candles.

2. Gaze at the flickering flames and take in their warmth. Think of them as the lights guiding you out of your situation and into freedom.

3. Imagine a string holding you down. Grab hold of it and say aloud:

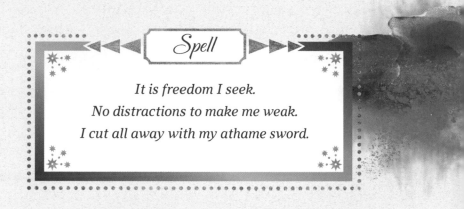

Spell

It is freedom I seek.
No distractions to make me weak.
I cut all away with my athame sword.

4. Now, cut the cord with your athame. Cut away whatever has been interfering with your life and let yourself be light.

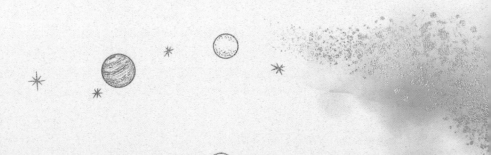

Honoring the Elements

The elements earth, air, fire, and water, and aether make up a pentacle, a ubiquitous symbol in witchcraft. Each point represents an element, and the highest point represents Spirit who watches over us. In this spell, you will perform an honorary ritual intended to show your gratitude.

Necessary components:

♦ 1 gray candle for air

♦ 1 brown candle for earth

♦ 1 blue candle for water

♦ 1 orange candle for fire

♦ 1 white candle for Spirit

♦ A computer with a printer

♦ Straight objects, like sticks or pens (optional)

1. From your computer, print a picture of a pentagram and place it on your altar. If you do not have a printer, you may use sticks or other straight objects to create the shape.

2. Arrange your altar so that the air candle sits on the point of the star that goes east. The earth candle sits on the approximate north direction, the water candle to the west, and the fire candle to the south. Spirit's aether candle is at the head of the pentacle.

3. Light each candle in the order issued above. For each element, say this quietly or aloud:

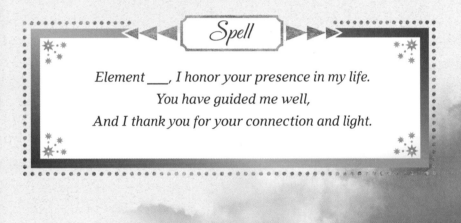

Spell

Element ___, I honor your presence in my life.
You have guided me well,
And I thank you for your connection and light.

Get on the Same Page

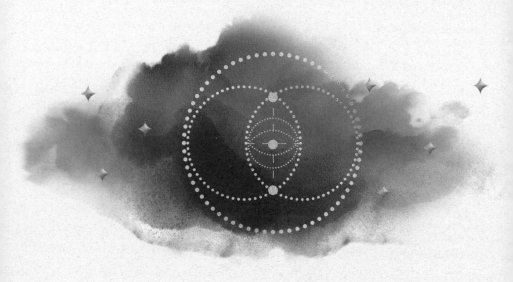

In sacred geometry there is a pattern, Vesica piscis, that is all about common ground. If you have been trying to get on the same page with someone but you can't, this spell will promote progress in understanding.

Necessary components:

♦ 3 pink candles for relationships

♦ A computer with a printer

♦ A pen

1. On your computer, find a picture of Vesica piscis and print it out.

2. Write your name on the left side of the Vesica piscis. On the right side, write the name of the person you are trying to come to terms with. In the middle, write down what you hope to resolve.

3. Place it on your altar and arrange the lit candles above what you have written.

4. Gaze into the candles. They are burning in harmony.

5. In your third eye, picture the two of you as independent forces. Then picture a bridge in between both of you. Walk toward each other until you are both in the middle. Now, picture what your relationship would look like if you were able to find some common ground. Hold on to that image and say quietly or aloud:

Spell

Vesica piscis, guide us.
We are meant to work together.
Show us the way.

6. Let the candles burn out.

Meditative Spiral Spell

The spiral is the most sacred of all shapes. Its movement can be seen in the twirl of a leaf, the movement of water, and within seashells. Because of its intrinsic ties to the earth, the spiral also has strong ties to the soul, and represents our spiritual journey. In this spell, you will use the power of the spiral to search for higher meaning and connection with the spiritual world.

Necessary components:

♦ 8 purple candles for Spirit

♦ A computer with a printer

1. Find a picture of the golden ratio spiral, print it out, and place it on your altar.

2. Arrange the lit candles so that they follow the pattern. Light the candles and gaze at the fire spiral before you.

3. Close your eyes and imagine the spiral moving outward and upward from you and into the air.

4. Now, picture that there is static electricity in the air, crackling and sparking up the energy spiral. Use it to attract the attention of your patron deity, angel, or Spirit, and listen.

After you have received their message, rest.

3

Crystal Magic

CRYSTALS ARE INTEGRAL IN magic and are an essential aspect of candle magic. Each crystal has their specific color, quality, and shape. Crystal magic is an excellent companion to candle magic because it combines so many elements like harmonizing colors or strengthening a witch's intuition. Unlike number magic, crystals are physical objects that can transmute energy from the crystal itself to the practitioner, connecting the two together.

If you are just venturing into crystal magic, clear quartz is perfect to start with. It can be a stand-in for all other crystals, and works in tandem with the colors of your candles.

Before starting any spells, make sure your crystals are cleansed and charged. There are a few ways to do this. You can let the crystals sit in salt overnight or let them soak in charged moon water. To charge them, you can leave them on your windowsill to absorb the sun or moonlight. Doing these steps will add more power and intention to any spell.

In this chapter, you will utilize the crystals to enhance your candle magic practice and manifest your desires.

Foster Compassion

One small moment of compassion can mean the difference between a horrible day and a shining one. With this spell, you will utilize the vibrations of celestite and cuprite to foster a more compassionate spirit.

Gather:

♦ 2 green candles for compassion

♦ Celestite for communicating with angels

♦ Cuprite for altruism

1. Arrange your altar with the candles and light them.

2. Rub your hands together to heat them up with internal energy.

3. Hold the celestite and the cuprite in your hands. Feel their energy.

4. Next, think of a situation where you were given grace. How did you feel prior to the help? Once you were helped, what was that feeling like? What are some ways you can pay kindness forward? Vow to put these thoughts into action.

Sardonyx, Give Us Strength

There are moments in our lives when we have been metaphorically beaten down by the pressures of our lives. We may be too tired to function or even take care of ourselves. But witches are not weak and helpless! We triumph. In this spell, you will borrow from sardonyx, a powerful agate, to find the willpower to move ahead. Note that this spell is meant to be supplemental to any other professional help you may need. Please seek out a medical professional if need be.

Gather:

♦ 1 yellow candle for willpower

♦ Sardonyx for strength

♦ 1 toothpick

1. On the yellow candle, inscribe 10 with the toothpick. This is the number of unity and completion. Light your candle.

2. Hold the sardonyx near the fire so that it warms but doesn't burn. Say quietly or aloud:

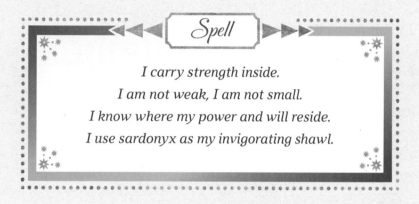

Spell

I carry strength inside.
I am not weak, I am not small.
I know where my power and will reside.
I use sardonyx as my invigorating shawl.

Banish Negative Energies

In witchcraft, we cultivate positivity for ourselves and others. But we can't be positive all the time, and an excess of negativity can bring a witch completely down. Use this spell to clear the negativity surrounding you.

Gather:

♦ 1 black candle

♦ Malachite for dispelling negativity

♦ Tape, a pen, and paper

♦ A small bowl of salt

1. Arrange your altar with the candle and light it. Let its presence act as a repellent for any lingering adversarial energies.

2. Hold the malachite and do a scan of your body, starting with the head downward.

3. Move about with your hand extended outward with the malachite in your upturned palm. Picture it sucking all the unwanted energies in the room and storing it inside.

4. Place it in a small bowl of salt so that it can purify overnight.

5. Finally, you will make a sigil that you will hang in your doorway. Write out the word "banish." From that word, remove the vowels so you are left with "bnsh." Draw out those letters in whatever way you want.

6. When you are done, tape the sigil to your doorframe or the door itself.

You have successfully banished the unwanted.
So mote it be.

Fortify Your Intuition

Intuition is that small voice telling us which direction we should go. We may neglect our intuition by putting our physical needs first, thereby ignoring our spiritual abilities. Intuition must be cultivated and practiced, otherwise it will wither. For this spell, open your third eye and look within yourself to find what you know is already there: your intuitive abilities.

Gather:

♦ 9 purple candles for intuition (or you can use 1 purple candle with a 9 carved on it)

♦ 1 toothpick (optional)

♦ 4 amethyst crystals

♦ Earplugs (optional)

♦ A mirror

1. Arrange your altar with the candles, then sit in a restful position.

2. Clear your mind of everything except the task at hand.

3. Whisper to the amethyst, *Show me the truth. Strengthen the voice inside me.*

4. Place the amethyst on the top of your head (crown chakra), forehead (third eye chakra), your throat (throat chakra), and your stomach (sacral chakra). These are all places where you might hear your intuition.

5. Ask the little voice inside you what it has to say. Do not overthink the response. Just listen. Take what they have said and stand before a mirror and say, *I am intuitive. It is in my nature. It is a part of who I am.*

Processing Broken Trust

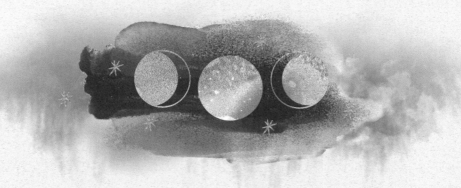

Humans are imperfect, and we might violate someone's boundaries without even realizing it. When we are on the receiving end of such a violation, it can be difficult to forgive. If we let distrust run our lives, we close ourselves off to the possibility of good. In this spell, you will start the journey to trust again.

Gather:

♦ 2 brown candles for trust

♦ 1 pink candle to represent the heart

♦ Amazonite for communication and openness

♦ A pen and your book of shadows

1. Arrange your altar by placing the candles in this order: brown, pink, brown. The first brown candle represents the trust you had that is now broken, and the second candle is the trust you wish to regain. The pink candle, representing your heart, sits in the middle as the key to the next step. Light the candles.

2. Hold the amazonite and your book of shadows; use the calming vibrations from the amazonite to think before you write anything down.

3. When you are ready, write the name of who violated your boundaries, what they did, and how that made you feel.

4. Ask yourself three questions. One: Is this the first time they have hurt you? Two: Do you think they deserve some grace? Three: Is your reaction proportional to the hurt?

Depending on the answers, you will know whether to move forward with this person or if you are better off without them. Trust your intuition and you will know what to do next.

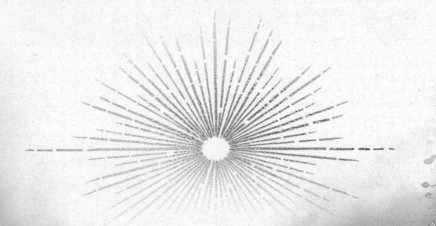

Get Creative with Sadv

Sadv is the Irish goddess of water and creativity. She is the mother of a poet and an inhabitant of the woodlands. According to legend, she created the forests. Her work can be seen in the rustle of the leaves or the tenderness of a doe. In this spell, you will call upon her to help your creative juices flow so that you can create masterpieces as Sadv did.

Gather:

♦ 3 orange candles for creativity

♦ Pieces of the forest, like leaves, twigs, or rocks

♦ A red robe (similar to Sadv)

1. Arrange your altar with the candles and light them.

2. Hold your foliage and feel the smoothness of the leaves, the chipping bark of the twigs. Say this aloud:

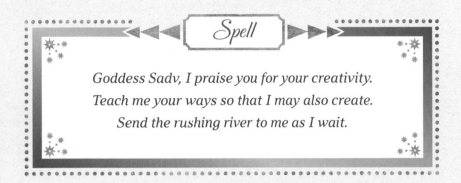

Spell

Goddess Sadv, I praise you for your creativity.
Teach me your ways so that I may also create.
Send the rushing river to me as I wait.

Now that you have called upon her name, feel the refreshing waters wash over you. Create your own forest in your mind and the spiritual world. Move about feeling carefree and just *be*.

Reconnect with Friends

If your social life has waned and you desire to rekindle your friendships, turn to this spell. In it, you will use the attracting power of the lodestone to draw your friends closer to you, and you to them.

Gather:

♦ At least 2 pink candles for friendship

♦ Lodestone for fortifying relationships

♦ Mementos of your pals

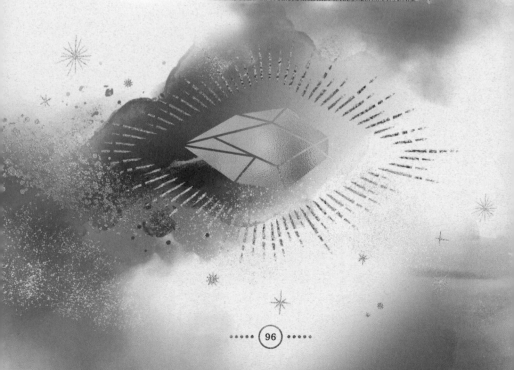

1. Arrange your altar with the mementos. Hold them in your hands and think fondly on what memories they bring you. Then, set up your candles and light them. Feel the glow from the candles as if it is inside you, warming your heart.

2. Place the lodestone near each memento for a few brief moments. You will want the energy to transfer from them to the stone.

3. Place the stone in front of the candles. As you do so, imagine the friend(s) you would like to spend some more time with. Concentrate on that and touch the stone to your heart. Let it feel the weight of your intention. Say this incantation aloud:

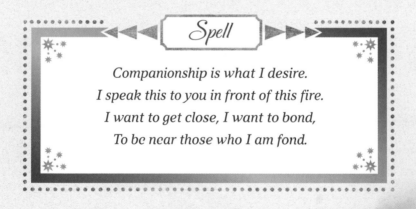

Spell

Companionship is what I desire.
I speak this to you in front of this fire.
I want to get close, I want to bond,
To be near those who I am fond.

Rekindle the Spark

If you feel as though your love life needs some extra verve, turn to this spell. In it, you will combine the passion of red and the inherent affection in rose quartz.

Gather:

♦ At least 3 red candles for romantic love

♦ 1 toothpick

♦ 2 pieces of rose quartz to represent you and your partner

♦ At least 1 picture of you and your beloved

♦ A bowl of sugar for sweet love

♦ Rose petals (optional)

1. Arrange your altar with the pictures. Decorate them and sprinkle the altar with rose petals, then place the bowl of sugar at the center of the altar and sprinkle some of it around.

2. Inscribe your initials on one candle and the initials of your beloved on another, leaving the candle in the middle unlit. Only light two of them.

3. Turn your attention to your pictures and ask yourself what made you fall in love in the first place. What was the initial attraction? What do you love about this person? Also, ask yourself what has caused your connection to fizzle out? Answer honestly. As you answer these questions, taste a bit of sugar.

4. Next, look at the flames dancing separately. Imagine you and your love on two opposing sides with the desire to get closer.

5. Take the two lit candles and light the one in the center, uniting you and your lover.

6. Now, hold the rose quartz close to your heart, and tell the Universe what you desire.

7. Once you are done, let all three candles burn out.

Comfort from Stress

When you feel as though you cannot get a moment of peace, it is time to make peace for yourself. This spell will help you carve out a moment to relax and breathe.

Necessary components:

♦ At least 1 blue candle for calm

♦ Jade for peace

♦ Soft music (optional)

♦ A stuffed animal to cuddle (optional)

1. Arrange your altar with items that make you smile. If you wish, turn on some music and cuddle up with your stuffed animal friend. Place and light the candle slowly.

2. Hold the jade firmly, but not too tight.

3. Take three deep breaths, inhale for 4 seconds, hold it for 4, and then exhale for 4.

4. Hold the jade to your belly, near your sacral chakra, and imagine it infusing you with calming energy. Let it spread through your abdomen and up your arms, then down your legs to your toes, to your heart, and all the way up to your head.

5. Breathe in one last time and let all the anxiety and stress leave you as you breathe out.

Strive to Thrive

We are meant to succeed and live happy, content lives. With this spell, focus on yourself and what you need to flourish in your life. Using calcite, you will open your mind to success.

Gather:

♦ At least 1 green candle for prosperity

♦ Calcite for opening your mind to new ways to succeed

♦ A small living plant (or seeds) to represent you

♦ Your book of light (or diary) and a pen

1. Arrange your altar with your favorite plant or seeds.

2. Place the calcite on the altar in the center. Hover your hands near your heart and gather energy there. Take as much as you need. Because the plant is meant to represent you, hover your hands over it and transfer the energy from you into the plant.

3. Next, hold the calcite in your hands and let it inspire you. Ask what you need to thrive, and be open to listen.

4. When an idea comes to you, write it down in your book of light while holding the crystal. Let it guide you.

5. Once your mind has been opened, put the calcite in front of the plant and let them touch.

6. Last, light the candle and let it burn out as close to the plant as possible.

You are on your way!

Nightmares No More

The presence of nightmares may be temporary, or they may be a clue of an underlying condition like stress or fatigue. Some believe that nightmares are a result of demons playing with your sleep. Whatever the reason, they must end, and this spell can help banish any malevolent spirits thwarting your good night.

Gather:

♦ At least 1 black candle for banishing (you may add more depending on the severity of your nightmares)

♦ Jet for dispelling nightmares

♦ Sage

1. Before you begin, cleanse your bedroom with sage, then arrange your altar with the candle and light it. Ensure the only light in the space is the candle. This may feel scary at first, but trust that the light will guide you through this night.

2. Hold the jet to your forehead, just above your third eye chakra. Continue to hold it there and envision it removing the stress, worries, or whatever else is causing you to have these bad dreams.

3. Next, hold the jet near the fire to burn away what it has taken from you. Be very careful that you do not burn yourself. When the crystal has been sufficiently heated, recite this incantation aloud:

Spell

Keep me safe and pure of thought
so I may sleep as I ought.

4. Let the candle burn out and place the jet underneath your pillow as you sleep.

Manifesting Your Dreams

The beauty of witchcraft is that it gives us the key to unlocking our dreams and, through the Universe, bring them to fruition. With this spell, you will conjure your desires, using blue lace agate to effectively communicate your dreams to Spirit.

Necessary components:

◆ At least 1 gray candle for manifesting

◆ Blue lace agate for communicating your desires

◆ A pen and notecards

◆ A comfortable place to sit

1. Before arranging your altar, take a moment to write your dreams down, one per card.

2. Prioritize which dreams are more urgent and eliminate any that are not. When you have whittled down the list, pick one major dream that you want to see fulfilled.

3. Add your candle to the altar and light it. Sit comfortably and take two deep breaths.

4. Next, hold the blue lace agate to your heart and voice box. This activates your chakras, enabling you to speak clearly. Place the agate on the notecard, then clearly state your dreams. Recite:

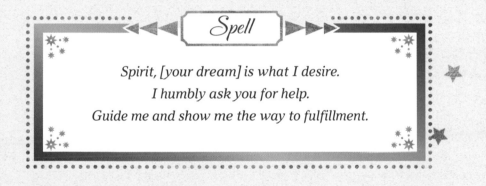

Spell

Spirit, [your dream] is what I desire.
I humbly ask you for help.
Guide me and show me the way to fulfillment.

5. Place the card somewhere you will see it every day and blow out the candle.

Prepare for Family Time

As much love as we have for our families, they can get on our nerves. If you are preparing to see your family for an extended period of time, let the healing power of zircon assist you. In this spell, you will prepare your spirit with the right attitude to face your family in harmony.

Gather:

♦ At least 1 pink candle for familial relationships

♦ 1 yellow candle for joy

♦ Zircon for stress

♦ Your favorite drink

♦ A picture of your family

1. Enjoy the drink before you begin. When you are done, arrange your altar with the yellow candle and pink candle. Light the yellow one first to promote a positive association with your family. Next, light the pink candle. After that, position the picture so you can see it near the candles.

2. Place the zircon near your root chakra. Let the zircon sit there for a moment so that it can radiate anti-stress vibrations through you.

3. Gaze at the picture. Your family cares for you and you for them. Meditate on this for a moment, and do not anticipate the ways they might annoy you. Just enjoy this time and think the best of them. When you are ready, blow out the candle and make your way to them.

Grounding Candle Spell

This grounding spell will remind you of what's important—you, the here, and the now.

Gather:

♦ 1 brown candle for grounding

♦ Petrified wood

1. Go outside to a place where you will not be disturbed. Next, take the candle(s) and arrange it however you'd like on your portable altar. If possible, take off your shoes so you can feel Mother Earth below you. If not, hold on to some nearby plant life.

2. Take several deep breaths until you feel calm and relaxed.

3. Light the candle and grip the petrified wood.

4. Close your eyes and use your senses. Smell the air, move your extremities, feel the sun or moonlight on your skin, and feel the texture of the wood. Empower yourself by saying:

◄◄◄ *Spell* ►►►

Nothing exists right now besides me and the present.
I am here, I am real, and I am content.

Ground Yourself in Reality

Panic and stress are masters at making us disassociate with our bodies and our reality. With this spell, you will find the tools you need to stay present in your body and your world.

Gather:

♦ 1 brown candle for grounding

♦ Red jasper for connection to the earth

1. Arrange your altar with the brown candle and light it. Think of it as your beacon; as long as you can see it, you are present.

2. Hold the jasper in your hands and take multiple deep breaths until you're calm. When you feel steady in these two areas, say aloud:

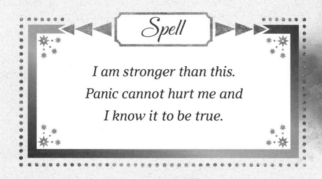

Spell

I am stronger than this.
Panic cannot hurt me and
I know it to be true.

Repeat until you feel better and know you are safe.

Guidance from the Universe

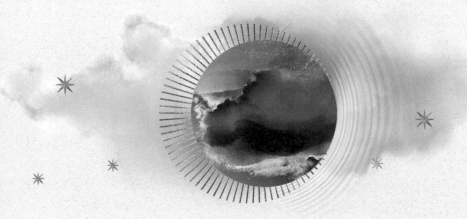

There is no shame in asking for help from anyone, especially the Divine. The Universe has its own plan, but it's also on your side! If you have been struggling for answers but do not know where to turn, utilize this spell and the communicative power of larimar.

Gather:

♦ At least 1 purple candle for guidance

♦ A larimar pendulum for communication

♦ A piece of paper or notecard and a pen

1. Before you begin, take the pendulum by the chain and hover the larimar over your hand. Ask the Universe to show you which direction means yes. Once it has shown you, do the same with the words "no," "maybe," and "unknown."

2. Write each word twice, opposite of each other, and place the paper before the lit candle.

3. Hold the pendulum so that the point hovers over the paper. Test the pendulum by asking it easily verifiable questions, like, "Is today Tuesday?" When you have calibrated it, ask for what you wish to know and say these words aloud:

Spell

O, Universe, hear my plea.
Show me what I must see.

Attune Your Focus

The world is littered with distractions. Focus is a necessary gift we must give ourselves and the spiritual world. If you're struggling to focus, this spell is right for you.

Gather:

- 1 orange tea candle for focus
- Smoky quartz
- Charged water
- A cauldron

1. Pour the charged water into your cauldron about halfway. You do not want to be able to see the candle, just its glow.

2. After you make sure there is no water on the candle, light it, then turn off or cover all other light sources. Sit in a comfortable position and gaze into the light.

3. Next, take the smoky quartz and place it on the top of your head. Think about what you need to pay attention to that you aren't. What does the light represent to you? What is another thing you need to focus on that you can't right now?

4. Take all this in and let everything else melt away until all you can think of is the important matter.

5. Once you feel calm and centered, blow out the candle, turn on the lights, and act on this new found focus.

4

Herbal Magic

HERBS CONNECT US TO THE Earth in the same way that candles connect us to the element of fire. Cultivating plants requires dedication, passion, knowledge, and respect for Mother Nature. It is very important to see the earth as having its own spirit, so do not act entitled to her resources. When gathering the proper herbs to pair with your candle spell, do everything possible to be conscientious and sustainable, and only buy locally. Growing your own herbs is even better because your time, energy, and care will enhance your spells exponentially.

Herbs have been a part of witchcraft since the practice began. Since the invention of agriculture hundreds of years ago, plants and nature have been a huge part of human life. Because of the technological advances of today, we are less connected to Mother Nature than we have ever been. Herbal magic is so special because it gives us a taste of what is possible, especially when paired with the element of fire in candle magic.

In this chapter, you will use herbal energies in your practice, not only to manifest your desires but also to teach you the different combinations that you can add to your practice. You may not have all the herbs listed, and that is okay! Rosemary can be a stand-in for any herb you lack. Go forth and get in touch with Nature.

Set the Mood

Love is the most powerful force, and physical intimacy enhances it. In this spell, you will channel your inner beguiler and set the mood for some intimacy.

Gather:

♦ 5 red candles for passion

♦ 5 pink candles for romantic love

♦ Damiana for attraction

♦ Rose petals for romance

♦ Jasmine to heighten desire

♦ Charged water

♦ A tea strainer and a diffuser

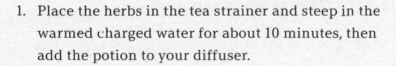

1. Place the herbs in the tea strainer and steep in the warmed charged water for about 10 minutes, then add the potion to your diffuser.

2. Decorate your bedroom with the candles and light them.

The most important part of setting the mood is being in the mood. When your lover comes over, make your move and have a great time.

Protective Herbal Coating

Paired with a black candle, this herbal coating will add an extra safeguard against those who may aim to do you harm.

Gather:

- ♦ At least 1 black candle
- ♦ Aloe gel as the base
- ♦ Lavender for peace
- ♦ Dill to keep away dark forces
- ♦ Basil to drive out hostile spirits
- ♦ Chia seeds for protection
- ♦ Bay leaf for protection
- ♦ Black pepper to banish spirits who may already be near
- ♦ A cleansed vessel for mixing the herbs
- ♦ A wooden spoon
- ♦ A pen
- ♦ A fireproof dish

1. Before you begin, call upon your deity to aid you.

2. Mix all the herbs in the vessel—except the bay leaf. Feel the textures and imagine the herbs giving you a warm but sturdy shield that fully encompasses you. Add the aloe gel and mix with the spoon.

3. As you work, recite this spell quietly or aloud:

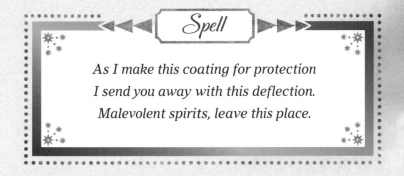

Spell

As I make this coating for protection
I send you away with this deflection.
Malevolent spirits, leave this place.

4. Once your ingredients are mixed, coat your black candle with the mixture.

5. Light your candle, then pause to watch the flames put your spell into action.

6. Write your name on the bay leaf, then put the leaf to the fire and let it burn out in a flameproof dish.

Take this time to conjure the power of your spiritual team, imagining them covering you in a bubble of light. This is your shield.

Coping with Sorrow

There are no words to fully encompass sorrow. In order to move on from pain, you must experience it. In this spell, you will give yourself the space to feel your emotions, however raw they may be. Give yourself room and you will heal.

Gather:

♦ 4 white candles for healing

♦ Your favorite incense

♦ Charged drinking water

♦ Sage to clear sadness

♦ Calamint to soothe sorrow

♦ Peace lily to pull you out of sadness

♦ Sugar

♦ A tea strainer

♦ A teacup

♦ An object that calms you

1. First, light the incense and let its scent float around you.

2. Boil the charged water and put the herbs in the tea strainer. Let them steep in the teacup for about 5 minutes.

3. Arrange your altar with the white candles and light them.

4. Next, grab your tea and take it in the room with you. You may have a few sips if you like, then hold your calming object and sit quietly.

5. Without holding back, let everything out. You may sit quietly, or you may cry immediately. Whatever feels right to you in that moment, do it. Then, when you have emptied yourself, drink the tea slowly. Feel it going down your throat and warming you from the inside.

Send Me Wisdom

Sometimes we are in difficult situations where the solution is not clear, or we feel lost and are unsure of what to do next. In this spell, you will petition Spirit for the answers you seek.

Gather:

- ♦ 2 purple candles for understanding
- ♦ Sage for wisdom
- ♦ Sunflower for wishes
- ♦ Lilac for spiritual aid
- ♦ A cauldron (preferably with a lid)
- ♦ 1 tablespoon of Epsom salt
- ♦ 1 tablespoon of rubbing alcohol
- ♦ Sand
- ♦ Oven mitts
- ♦ A spoon

1. Place the candles somewhere in your space—but not on the altar—and light them.

2. Put the cauldron on top of the fireproof surface. Pour the Epsom salt inside, then add the herbs.

3. Pour the rubbing alcohol in and mix them all together. Keep the sand, oven mitts, and lid at the ready, just in case you need them. Light a match and drop it into the cauldron, ensuring it lies flat.

4. Now wait for the fire to catch on the rubbing alcohol. You will hear sputtering, and then the fire will grow about twice as high as the cauldron. When the flames have risen, recite this incantation aloud:

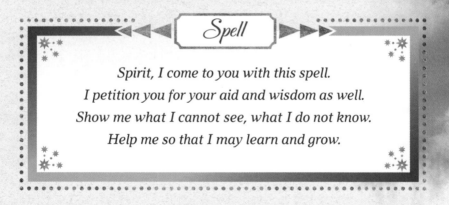

Spell

Spirit, I come to you with this spell.
I petition you for your aid and wisdom as well.
Show me what I cannot see, what I do not know.
Help me so that I may learn and grow.

5. Wait for the fire to go out, or put the lid on the cauldron to snuff out the fire. Now listen closely for what Spirit has to say.

Happy, Happy Sachet

As witches, it is important to maintain our sense of happiness. With this spell, you will use the power of candles and herbal magic to infuse happiness throughout your day.

Gather:

- ◆ 2 orange candles for happiness
- ◆ 2 yellow candles for joy
- ◆ A small sachet bag
- ◆ Bee pollen for high spirits
- ◆ Anise to find happiness
- ◆ Dried orange peel for attracting joy
- ◆ Azalea for gaiety
- ◆ A pen and a small piece of paper

1. Fill the sachet bag with the herbs. You can eyeball how much of each herb you would like because it is all about what *you* want and what *you* will enjoy. Use your intuition.

2. Once you are done filling the sachet, take your pen and write a sigil with the word "contentment" on your small piece of paper. Place it in the sachet.

3. Arrange the candles in a circle, alternating between the colors. Place the sachet in the circle and then light the candles.

4. Sit back, place your hands in a prayer position and bring them to your heart's center. Recite this incantation quietly or aloud:

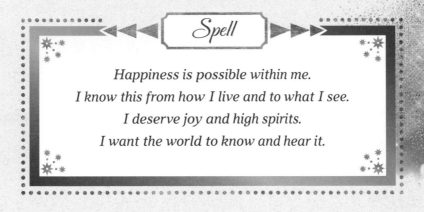

Spell

Happiness is possible within me.
I know this from how I live and to what I see.
I deserve joy and high spirits.
I want the world to know and hear it.

Take the sachet with you wherever you go, and don't forget to smile!

Show Me the Money

As much as we may dislike it, the world revolves around money. We need it to survive, live, have fun—almost everything. Many of us don't have as much as we want or even as much as we need, yet we still must carry on. But we do not have to do so on our own! Instead, we can petition the Universe to give us the money we need and deserve. With this spell, you will call on the Universe to bless you with cash.

Gather:

- ◆ 1 green candle for abundance
- ◆ Coins
- ◆ The Ten of Pentacles tarot card for financial success
- ◆ Allspice for money
- ◆ Basil to attract success
- ◆ Blackberry for attracting money

1. Arrange your altar with the candle and light it.

2. Place the Ten of Pentacles on the altar and put one finger on it. This will connect you to your future wealth.

3. Next, sprinkle some coins atop the altar and keep some in your hand. Delight in the ring of the coins as they hit the table. This is the sound you crave, and this will let the Universe know what you are calling for.

4. Now take the herbs and eat them one by one. This will make your body part of the attraction.

5. Once eaten, take the coins in your hand and shake them about, making as much noise as is comfortable. Sing this aloud:

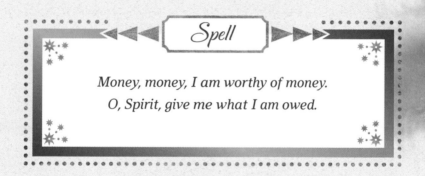

Spell

Money, money, I am worthy of money.
O, Spirit, give me what I am owed.

Repeat as many times as necessary and wait for your reward.

Ancestral Offerings

Your ancestors know you well and have your best interests at heart. What better way to petition their help than with an ancestral offering in exchange for their blessing?

Gather:

- ◆ At least 1 white candle for benedictions
- ◆ St. John's wort for blessings
- ◆ A blessed vessel
- ◆ A pen and your book of light
- ◆ Paint and a paint brush (optional)
- ◆ A canvas (optional)

1. Arrange your altar with the white candle and light it.

2. Fill the vessel with St. John's wort, then touch the herb and swirl it around in a deosil (clockwise) motion. This will embed your energy and essence into the herbs, further connecting you to your ancestors.

3. Write a song or a poem, then sing it aloud. In the same tune, recite this incantation:

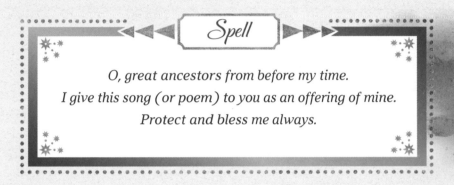

Spell

O, great ancestors from before my time.
I give this song (or poem) to you as an offering of mine.
Protect and bless me always.

If you prefer painting to poetry, make a small painting for your ancestors to show them your dedication to them. Ask them for whatever blessing you desire, and when you are done, leave your offerings on a dedicated altar to your ancestors.

Dispel Dark Emotions

There are some periods in our lives when we are sucked down into a hole of negative emotions. It is completely normal to not feel happy or positive, but if it continues for an extended period of time, magic must step in. In this ritual, you will dispel the dark emotions that have plagued you.

Gather:

♦ 6 black candles for banishing

♦ Ground coffee

♦ A tarp for easy cleanup

1. Place the tarp on the ground and arrange the black candles in a large circle, then light them.

2. Sprinkle the ground coffee in a circle within the candle circle.

3. Sit inside the circles and focus on yourself. Where are the negative emotions coming from? Your heart, your stomach? Focus on that area and hold your hands to it.

4. Picture your negative feelings flowing out of you and into your hands. Then, spread them out over the coffee circle. The coffee will help rid you of this pain. Recite this binding spell quietly or aloud:

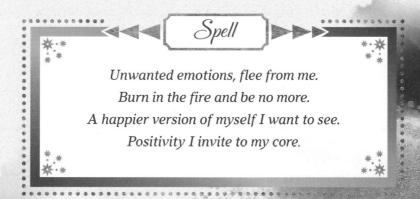

Spell

Unwanted emotions, flee from me.
Burn in the fire and be no more.
A happier version of myself I want to see.
Positivity I invite to my core.

Bind Malevolent Spirits

Spirits are everywhere: In Nature, in our homes, and in the outside world. There are those who desire to help us, and those who mean to do us harm. In this spell, you will learn to bind and release any evil that has come into your life.

Gather:

♦ 7 black candles for banishment

♦ Vinegar for binding

♦ A blessed vessel

♦ A spoon

♦ A poppet

♦ A piece of string long enough to tie up the poppet

♦ Rubber gloves

1. Arrange your candles on your altar in a horizontal line, then light them.

2. Place the vessel on the altar, then slowly pour the vinegar into it.

3. Stir the vinegar in a deosil (clockwise) motion 7 times to activate its power.

4. Next, make your poppet. A poppet is a stand-in for another being, similar to a voodoo doll. It can be made out of anything and can be any shape you wish. For this spell, make sure your poppet is something you can tie a string around.

5. Now, tie the poppet with the string and then recite these words aloud:

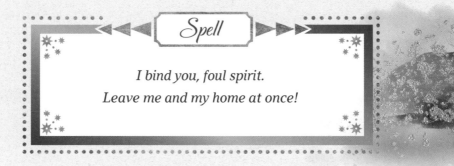

Spell

I bind you, foul spirit.
Leave me and my home at once!

6. Put your rubber gloves on and dip the poppet into the vinegar, ensuring it is fully submerged.

7. Stir the vinegar another seven times in a widdershins (counterclockwise) motion to take the spirit's power away.

8. When the poppet has fully soaked through, pour the vinegar outside as a libation, and discard the poppet.

Enlightening Oil

Anointing oil is used to add an extra layer of intention to any candle spell. This spell is meant for those who wish to gain enlightenment in a particular area or to improve their psychic abilities.

Gather:

♦ 1 purple or white candle

♦ Anise star

♦ Celery seeds

♦ Cinnamon

♦ Lemon balm

♦ Mexican saffron

♦ 1 or 2 amethyst chips

♦ Base oil (such as olive, jojoba, grapeseed, or almond oil)

♦ 1 blessed and cleansed vessel to mix the ingredients

♦ 1 cleansed and charged glass container

1. In the vessel, stir the herbs in a deosil (clockwise) motion to activate their magical properties.

2. Blow on the amethyst chips to infuse them with your energy, then dump them into the herbal mix.

3. Pour some of your oil into its new glass container, then alternate between the oil and the enchanted herb mixture.

4. Once full, shake it in your hand three times to represent your past, present, and what you will discover in the future.

5. Coat the candles in anointing oil, and whisper:

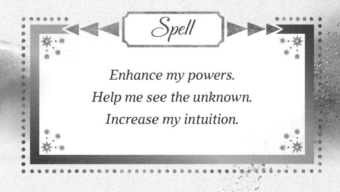

Spell

Enhance my powers.
Help me see the unknown.
Increase my intuition.

6. Light the candle and imagine your mind being covered with light the way knowledge illuminates our consciousness.

7. Close your eyes and open your third eye. Imagine an antenna coming from the top of your head, waiting to receive a message from the Universe. It is all right if nothing comes to you right away. Give it some time and be patient.

Purify Your Home

A home can become unclean with the negative energy of others, the presence of unwanted spirits, or even our own negative energy permeating the walls. As a witch, you are empowered enough to do something about it. In this spell, you will cleanse your entire home from the inside out.

Gather:

♦ 6 white candles for cleansing

♦ Sage to burn

♦ A cauldron

♦ Black salt

♦ A small, charged container for the salt

1. First, place the black salt in the charged container and take it outside with you. Pour the salt around the perimeter of your home. This will prevent malevolent spirits and energies from entering.

2. Next, place the sage inside your cauldron.

3. Light a match and drop it into the cauldron, ensuring it does not go out before burning the leaves. When the sage starts to burn, carry the cauldron with you throughout the house. Let the smoke touch every possible corner. As you move about, recite:

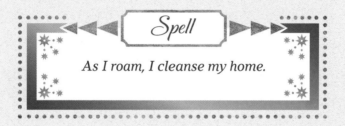

Spell

As I roam, I cleanse my home.

4. Say this over and over until you have finished the ritual. Repeat as needed.

Adjusting to Transitions

It has been said that change is the only constant in life. Throughout our lives we go from infant to child, young adult to adult, and then to elder. We *are* change. Even so, there are some changes that are frightening, like looking for a new job or having a child. This ritual will help you have confidence in yourself and adjust to the changes in your life.

Gather:

- ◆ 5 gray candles for change
- ◆ Peppermint leaves
- ◆ Charged drinking water
- ◆ A charged bowl
- ◆ A blessed vessel
- ◆ A tea strainer
- ◆ Incense (optional)

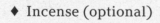

1. Before you begin, take the peppermint leaves, and put them in the tea strainer. Let steep in the charged water for 10 minutes.

2. Arrange the candles on the altar and light them. If you are using incense, light it now.

3. When the peppermint is done seeping, remove it and toss it outside. Take the water and transfer it to the vessel. Carry it with you back to the altar.

4. Set the concoction on the altar, and then hold your hands to your heart center. Take some deep breaths and calm yourself.Once you are breathing fine and you are at peace, recite these words aloud:

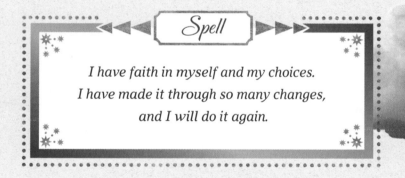

Spell

I have faith in myself and my choices.
I have made it through so many changes,
and I will do it again.

5. Now, take a sip of the water as you complete the ritual. Carry the potion with you and take sips whenever you are feeling nervous or unsure.

Wind Down

If there is too much stress in our systems, it can clog our chakras and prevent us from living life as our fullest selves. When we cannot live as ourselves, we become disconnected not only from our craft, but also from the people around us. It can be very isolating, but you must resist, and this spell will help.

Gather:

- 3 blue candles for calm
- 3 green candles for peace
- Lavender
- Chamomile
- Passionflower
- A mortar and pestle
- A teapot
- Charged water
- A cauldron
- Grapeseed oil
- A spoon

1. Grind the herbs in the mortar and pestle without getting them to a fine powder.

2. Pour about 1 teaspoon of grapeseed oil into your cauldron, and then mix in the herbs in a deosil (clockwise) motion.

3. Boil the charged water. Once it is ready, take the teapot into your workspace.

4. Arrange the candles in whichever order you want and light them.

5. Next, slowly pour the water into the cauldron. Be careful, as the water will be hot. Put your face over the cauldron, and breathe in the scent of the water. Let it soothe you and calm you.

Sit back and let the smell permeate the room and take a moment to stare at the candles. Watch their movements and get lost in a trance. Let your mind turn blank and *relax*.

Break That Hex

If one is to curse another, it is to intentionally hurt them for an extended period of time. A hex is a kind of curse, but it is weaker and shorter. If you believe someone has been deliberately trying to harm you with negative energies, you might have been hexed. Use this spell to reverse any hex cast upon you.

Gather:

♦ 1 black candle for breaking the hex

♦ 1 white candle to purify the space

♦ Grapeseed oil (or olive oil) as the base

♦ Dried peony leaves for protection against negativity

♦ Dried angelica to remove the hex

♦ Dried blessed thistle for purification

♦ A mortar and pestle

♦ A blessed vessel, long and wide enough to roll the candles in

1. Before getting started, take several deep breaths. Once your emotions are neutral, you may proceed.

2. Take the dried herbs and grind them in the mortar and pestle so that they easily stick to the oil.

3. Pour the oil inside the vessel and sprinkle the herbs on top.

4. Roll the black candle in the mixture.

5. Next, go to your altar with the candle and place it in the middle. Wash your hands clean, and then light the candle. Say quietly or aloud:

Spell

I send this hex away.
Far gone for another day.
May it find its sender
And make them vulnerable and tender.

6. Let the black candle burn down and imagine it as if you are burning the hex.

7. Light the white candle and let it burn down.

It's Your Lucky Day

Luck, we can all use more of it. If you have been experiencing a series of misfortunes, or you simply need a boost, this spell will help you conjure the fortune you need.

Gather:

♦ 1 green candle for luck

♦ 1 silver candle for manifestation

♦ 1 lucky object like a coin or a card (or an object you would like to make lucky)

♦ Catnip for luck

♦ Chamomile for increased fortune

♦ A blessed bowl

1. Start the spell by taking the chamomile and the bowl into the washroom with you. Turn on the water and ensure it is either warm or hot.

2. Deposit the chamomile into the bowl and add the water. Let the chamomile steep, then wash your hands with the concoction. Dry your hands and return to your workspace.

3. Arrange your altar with the candles and light them. Hold your lucky object in your hands.

4. Next, put it on the altar and sprinkle catnip on your item. As you do so, say quietly or aloud:

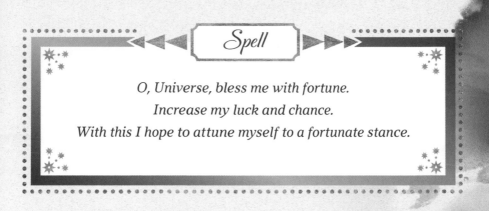

Spell

O, Universe, bless me with fortune.
Increase my luck and chance.
With this I hope to attune myself to a fortunate stance.

5. Carry the object with you wherever you go.

Offering to Mother Moon

Mother Moon watches over us every night as she makes her ascent into the star-filled sky. With her light, we can see at night, rather than be completely covered by darkness. She changes her appearance at times from a big yellow ball to a glimmering silver entity. Mother Moon is beautiful. She does so much for us without asking for anything in return. For this alone, she is worthy of praise. Send her a message of gratitude.

Wait to perform this spell during the Full Moon when Mother is at her brightest and most energetic. If possible, go outside for this spell or, alternatively, perform it by a windowsill in view of the Full Moon.

Gather:

♦ 1 silver candle to represent Mother Moon

♦ 1 gray candle to represent you

♦ Lettuce, cabbage, and pumpkin for lunar magic

♦ A blessed bowl

♦ Charged moon water in a blessed vessel

1. Before performing the spell, charge your moon water the night before so that it is fresh to use.

2. Next, cut up the vegetable herbs so that they all fit into the bowl.

3. Arrange your altar and light the silver candle first and then the gray candle.

4. Place the bowl on the altar, put your hands to your heart center, and close your eyes. Say this to Mother Moon:

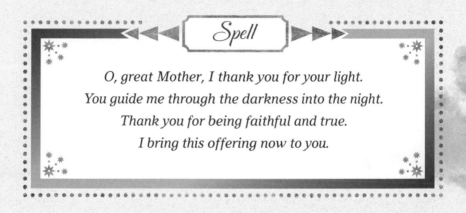

Spell

O, great Mother, I thank you for your light.
You guide me through the darkness into the night.
Thank you for being faithful and true.
I bring this offering now to you.

5. Leave the bowl on the altar overnight. In the morning, leave it outside for the animals to eat.

Restore Passion for Life

Our lives can very easily turn into a repetitive motion where we are no longer living but merely surviving. With this spell, reclaim your passion for life, and remember that you are alive! So mote it be.

Necessary components:

♦ 3 white candles to represent your mind, body, and soul

♦ 3 red candles to represent passion in those parts of the body

♦ Quick tempo music

♦ Workout attire or comfortable clothes

♦ A big enough space to move around

♦ A red piece of fabric (optional)

♦ Charged drinking water (optional)

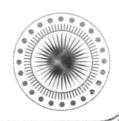

1. Arrange your altar with the candles.

2. Touch each white candle to your forehead, abdomen, and heart, then light them. Do the same with the red candles and light them.

3. Put on music and slowly lose yourself in it. Let your body move in whatever way you want. You may move slowly at first but pick up your pace and dance until you sweat. It is important that you feel the blood pumping in your veins and your breath speeding up. These are markers that you are *alive*.

4. If you choose, wave the red fabric in the air as wildly as you wish. Think of it as spreading your new invigorated passion through the air, staining it with color. When you are coming back down, take long gulps of the charged water.

You did it! You are real and you are here.

Conclusion

Congratulations! You are now a skilled candle magic practitioner. You have journeyed through colors, numbers, crystals, and herbs, and have come out more knowledgeable than ever before. Now that you have taken this journey, you are one step closer to mastering witchcraft. You have learned some of the color meanings, the mystical world of numerology and angel numbers, the power of crystals, and the healing power of herbs. These will be invaluable skills the longer you practice.

As you move forward on your witchy path, you may use this spell book however you please. Consider this book a template for any future spells you may encounter, or create on your own. The beauty of witchcraft is that it is completely customizable.

If you related to some parts of the spell but not others, change it! If the incantations were not your speed, rewrite them! You have the gift of doing whatever your intuition feels is right. Building on top of or altering spells is what makes spells *yours*, and that connects you to your craft and to yourself. You are in control, and from now on, you set the rules.

There are limitations in this book, as there are in many books, but this is a taste of what is to come. Next you may want to focus on strengthening your psychic abilities, or you may want to move on to the prophetic magic of tarot cards. The possibilities are endless for those who wish to learn and explore. Now take your newfound knowledge and go out into the world with a new perspective. May you continue to grow and flourish.

So Mote It Be.

Spell Index

First published in 2023, by Wellfleet Press, an imprint of The Quarto Group,
142 West 36th Street, 4th Floor, New York, NY 10018, USA
T (212) 779-4972 F (212) 779-6058 www.Quarto.com

Wellfleet titles are also available at discount for retail, wholesale, promotional,
and bulk purchase. For details, contact the Special Sales Manager by email at
specialsales@quarto.com or by mail at The Quarto Group, Attn: Special Sales
Manager, 100 Cummings Center Suite 265D, Beverly, MA 01915 USA.

10 9 8 7 6 5 4 3 2 1

ISBN: 978-1-57715-388-7

Library of Congress Control Number: 2023931594

Publisher: Rage Kindelsperger
Creative Director: Laura Drew
Managing Editor: Cara Donaldson
Editor: Sara Bonacum
Cover and Interior Design: Evelin Kasikov
Text: Johanie M. Cools

Printed in China

Continue your spellcraft with these additional companions:

978-1-57715-390-0

978-1-57715-391-7

978-1-57715-393-1

978-1-57715-389-4

978-1-57715-392-4